Remember these 32 Chinese Alphabets ?

1. Parallels	2. Dots (Left to Right)	3. 0Dots (Top to Bottom)	4. Final Dot	5. Half Ladder	6. T-Shape	7. Split	8. Vertical Split

9. Slide	10. Cross	11. 7-Slash Split	12. 7L-Hook Split	13. Marching	14. Tick	15. 7-Hook Flag	16. L-Beng Flag

17. 7-Hook Frame	18. U-Frame	19. C-Frame	20. Flipped-C	21. L7-Hook Frame	22. L7-Enclosure	23. n-Frame	24. Skewer
					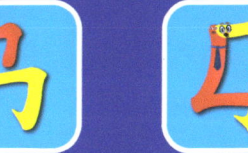		

25. Single Leg	26. Multiple Legs	27. Split Intersections	28. Tripod	29. Flat Intersections	30. Horizontals Enclosure	31. Verticals Enclosure	32. Intersections Enclosure

In this book, you will meet other members in their teams.

In a Chinese Alphabet,

the first stroke is **RED** ①

the second stroke is **YELLOW** ②

the third stroke is **BLUE** ③

the fourth stroke is **GREEN** ④

the fifth stroke is **ORANGE** ⑤

the sixth stroke is **PURPLE** ⑥

Parallels 1

三
three

须
feelers

川
river

巢
nest

② Dots (Left to Right)

六
six

火
fire

豹
leopard

菜
vegetables

黑
black

③ Dots (Top to Bottom)

飞
fly

雨
rain

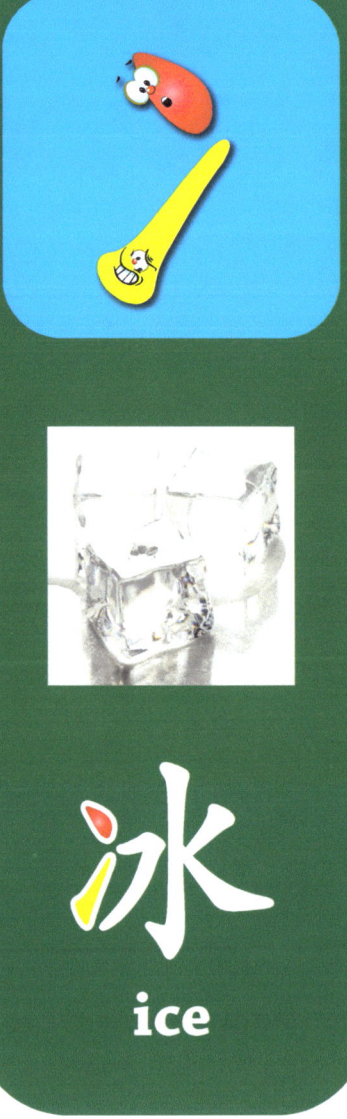
冰
ice

汁
juice

Final Dot

云 — cloud
西瓜 — water-melon
铃 — bell
橙 — orange

5 Half Ladder

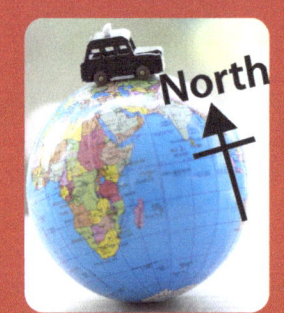

上 up

北 north

面 noodles

咖啡 coffee

排队 to queue

⑥ T-Shape

	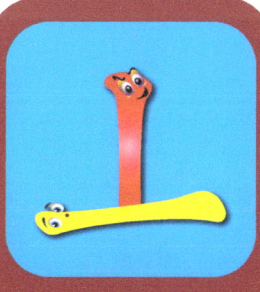				
			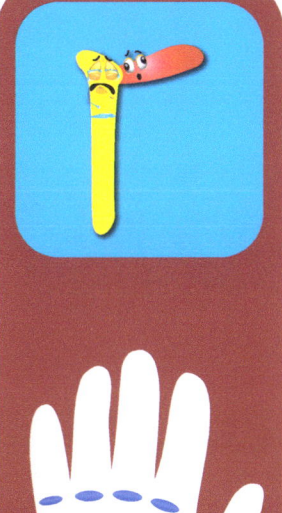		
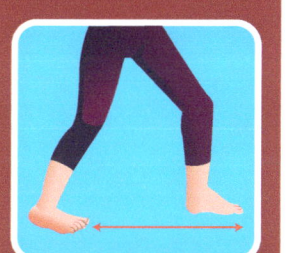					
一步	虫	五	手套	汤匙	亚军
one step	worm	five	glove	soup spoon	second place

⑦ Split

八
eight

人
people

茎
stalk

眨眼
wink

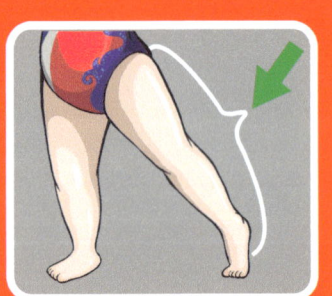
腿
leg

⑧ Vertical Split

花
flower

银行
bank

乒乓
table tennis

竹
bamboo

篮子
basket

Slide ⑨

水
water

手表
watch

凳子
stool

⑩ Cross

斧

axe

叉

fork

家庭

family

孑孓

wriggler

ㄉ-Slash ⑪

多
many

警察
police

冬天
winter

夜晚
night

⑫ 乙-Hook

玩具
toys

梳子
comb

飞机
aeroplane

九
nine

⑬ Marching

豺
jackal

矛
spear

狗
dog

象
elephant

Tick

礼物

gift

扫

to sweep

孑孓

wriggler

15 7-Hook Flag

爷爷

grandfather

衣服

clothes

太阳

sun

⑯ L-Bend Flag

回收桶
recycling bin

聊天
to chat

孩子
child

⑰ 7-Hook Frame

刀
knife

一万
ten thousands

巧克力
chocolate

羽毛
feather

(18) L-Frame & U-Frame

匕首
dagger

龙
dragon

画
painting

山
mountain

⑲ C-Frame

匚	二	匚	区	巨	臣

ability
administration
agency
beautiful
behaviour
campaign
candidate

芒果　牙　词汇　海鸥　巨大　宝藏

mango　teeth　vocabulary　seagull　huge　treasure

⑳ Flipped-C

尺
ruler

雪花
snow flake

糖果
sweets

巴士
bus

鹿
deer

21 - Hook

手铐	号码	写	马	乌鸦
handcuffs	numbers	to write	horse	crow

㉒ 凵-Enclosure

习惯
habits

喙
beak

母牛
cow

练习
practice

n-Frame

贝壳
shell

网
net

门
door

口
mouth

㉔ Skewer

降落伞
parachute

出口
exit

毛巾
towel

中间
middle

25 Single Leg

十	千	干	半	丰	羊

十
ten

饼干
biscuit

半
half

羊
sheep

蜂
bee

拜
to worship

(26) Multiple Legs

草
grass

领带
tie

舞
dance

开
to open

井
well

27 Split Intersections

big

sky

husband

webbed feet

baseball

Tripod (28)

wood

younger sister

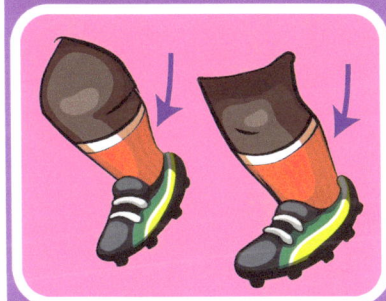

socks

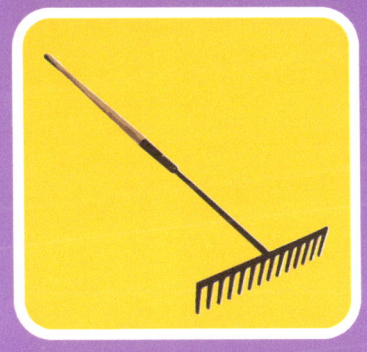

rake

㉙ Flat Intersections

土

earth

王

king

星星

star

香蕉

banana

蜡笔

crayon

瓶塞

bottle cap

30 Horizontals Enclosure

 月 moon

 日 sun

 眉 eyebrows

姐姐 elder sister

 直线 straight line

㉛ Verticals Enclosure

鸸鹋

emu

口罩

mask

栗子

chestnut

盒

box

32 Intersections Enclosure

	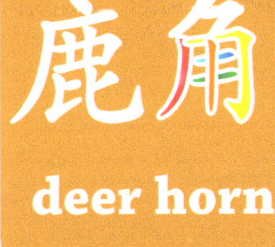				

鱼 — fish
柚子 — pomelo
鹿角 — deer horn
蝙蝠 — bat
歌曲 — song
字典 — dictionary

www.ingramcontent.com/pod-product-compliance
Lightning Source LLC
Chambersburg PA
CBHW042107050526

44107CB00108B/1213